THE YORKSHIRE DA RAILWAY
The Grassington Branch

One of the four locomotives employed by Hutchinson on the YDR constructional contract was WHH No. 3, an 0-6-0ST built by Manning Wardle in 1895. It was photographed "on the job" at the site of Ings Bridge, nr Linton. Ings Bridge was to be a charmingly eccentric stone footbridge (No. 37), carrying an ancient footpath from Linton to Threshfield across the line and is illustrated on page 27. Of interest is the switch-back track, mixture of low side and 5 plank railway wagons, contractors wagons and tools of the trade. WHH No. 3 is a typical Manning Wardle product of the 1890s and appears to be in clean condition. Unfortunately its livery is unknown but there is evidence of lining out.

D. Binns Collection.

1. EARLY PROPOSALS

Skipton was placed in rail contact with Leeds, Bradford and the South on 7 September 1847 when the Leeds & Bradford (Shipley–Colne Extension) Railway opened single track only between Keighley and Skipton. The Company were to extend to Colne so opening up a through route from the West Riding to Manchester and Liverpool. On 30 July 1849 the "little" North Western Railway opened part of its route from an end on junction with the Leeds & Bradford Railway at Skipton, to Clapham and Ingleton where work came to a halt. A change of plan brought the "little" North Western Railway to Lancaster on 1 June 1850 when passengers could travel by train from Skipton to Lancaster and Morecambe. At Lancaster, connection was effected with the Lancaster & Carlisle Railway thus forming a through route from the West Riding to Scotland. Both the Leeds and Bradford Railway along with its Shipley–Colne Extension and the "little" North Western Railway were destined to become part of the Midland Railway empire.

Over the years many proposals have been formulated for railways connecting the Midland Railway/Lancashire & Yorkshire Railway area around Hellifield and Skipton with the North East, running via Wharfedale, but none were to come to fruition. In 1845 the Lancashire & North Yorkshire Railway proposed 47½ miles of line from the Leeds & Bradford (Shipley–Colne branch) via Gargrave, Kettlewell, Buckden and Middleham to Scorton where it would connect with the Richmond branch. At the same time, the Liverpool, Manchester & Newcastle upon Tyne Railway was proposing similar schemes connecting Lancashire with the North East. It amalgamated with the Lancashire & North Yorkshire, the combined venture using the Liverpool, Manchester & Newcastle upon Tyne Railway title. The Royal Assent was given on 26 June 1846 with powers to construct a line passing through Grassington, Kettlewell and Buckden, then via Aysgarth and Catterick. This scheme required a tunnel more than 2 miles in length from near Cray to Bishopdale. The entire project was abandoned in January 1848.

A similar proposal was advertised locally about this same time by an un-named group for a line connecting Wensleydale and Wharfedale which would have required a long, deep tunnel near Buckden. Nothing further was heard from the promoters and the scheme slid into oblivion. Another proposal of the mid-1840s concerned a section of the proposed Leeds & Carlisle Railway which was absorbed into the Northern Counties Union Railway in 1846. The original Leeds & Carlisle proposal was for a line from Carlisle, following the Eden Valley to Garsdale Head, then turning east into Wensleydale, to Bainbridge, and from there forking south to Semerwater and Stalling Busk. The line was to be taken beneath Yockenthwaite Moor by a tunnel more than 3 miles long emerging near Hubberholme and then continuing south through Upper Wharfedale. The scheme was abandoned prior to 1846.

A new Company, the Skipton, Wharfedale & Leyburn Junction was preparing plans in readiness for the 1865 Parliamentary Session, proposing 31 miles of railway from the "little" North Western Railway at Gargrave station, running to Kettlewell and eventually joining the North Eastern Railway's Northallerton, Bedale & Leyburn branch near Spennithorne. If successful the SW&LJ would have encroached deep into NER territory and not unexpectedly they opposed this MR/LYR invasion. The outcome was the Skipton & Wharfedale Railway Act which was passed on 5 July 1865 for a line terminating at Grassington. The local concern unsuccessfully attempted to obtain powers for a northern extension in 1866 and 1867, but was abandoned in 1869.

A new Company—The Skipton & Kettlewell Railway came into being in 1879 intending a line from the Midland Railway at Gargrave, passing via Flasby, Hetton, Threshfield and Coniston to Kettlewell where it was to terminate in a field known locally as "Priests Rain". In April 1880 the Midland Railway had declined an invitation to work the line and local opposition ensured that the bill passed on 26 August 1880 was reduced to a 9 mile branch commencing near Gargrave and terminating at Threshfield. The Midland Railway had also refused permission for the Skipton & Kettlewell Company to run over its tracks from Gargrave to Skipton and Keighley. In the following year (1881) a Skipton & Kettlewell bill was before Parliament for a 9 mile northern extension via Coniston and Kettlewell, passing through Upper Wharfedale to Buckden, then tunnelling under Buckden Pike into Bishopdale, joining the North Eastern Railway's Wensleydale branch near Aysgarth. Running powers were requested over the NER to Leyburn and over the MR to Shipley. Not un-naturally both the MR and NER were not amused and the promoters withdrew their bill.

With typical Yorkshire grit the Skipton & Kettlewell Railway proposed an even more ambitious scheme in 1882—this time striking for the heart of the North Eastern Railway at Darlington. Predictably the bill failed.

In the same year a new Company—the North Yorkshire & Lancashire Railway, deposited its bill for 33 miles of line from Hellifield via Hetton, Linton, Threshfield, Kettlewell, before passing into Coverdale and forward to the NER in Wensleydale, along with two branches to the Skipton & Kettlewell, the existing powers of which it planned to acquire. Threatened once again, the NER objected and the NY&LR was not heard of again. Not so for the Skipton & Kettlewell promoters who in 1883 prepared a bill somewhat simplified in relation to the previous one, but still aimed at Darlington by means of 47 miles of line from Threshfield. Again unsuccessful, yet another S&K bill was before Parliament in 1884 to revive its land purchase powers of 1880 and also seeking to extend northwards from Threshfield in a manner somewhat similar to the 1881 proposal, joining the NER near Aysgarth. The Company was to change its name to the Skipton & North Eastern Junction Railway—but the bill was rejected and in the following year (1885) the S&K obtained an Act authorising abandonment of its 1880 line and the winding up of its affairs.

During the early 1890s thoughts were again turned to railway construction in Upper Wharfedale and a new scheme was suggested by some of the parties involved in the earlier Skipton & Kettlewell scheme. Sir Mathew Wilson, the first Baronet, had died in 1891 and had been succeeded by his first son Sir Matthew Wharton Wilson who declared his interest in a possible new railway. So too did Edgar Ferguson (Engineer), William Atkinson Procter, and George Kendall of Skipton (who had been Secretary of the Skipton, Wharfedale & Leyburn Junction in the mid-1860s). They were joined by Marmaduke D'Arcy Wyvill and Lieut Col William Wade Maude. The scheme put forward in 1895 was an ambitious project—the Yorkshire Dales Railway—for some 59 miles of line at an estimated cost of £1,489,207 connecting the LYR and MR at Hellifield and the MR south of Embsay (on the Skipton–Ilkley line), with the NER at Darlington. A line some 7 miles long was to run in an easterly direction from a double junction at Hellifield, joining a 4 mile long line from Embsay at Rylstone, before proceeding northwards via Threshfield, Coniston and Kettlewell, then passing through a 6000yd long tunnel under Great Whernside (north east of Arncliffe) to bring the line into Coverdale. The route was then via Middleham, Spenithorne, Leyburn and Richmond, joining the NER south of Darlington. In connection with this proposal, running powers were sought over the MR to Hellifield, Skipton and Ilkley, over the LYR branch from Hellifield to Blackburn, and over the NER to Darlington and Middlesbrough. The bill was withdrawn by the promoters and the Yorkshire Dales scheme re-planned. Later that year the Company was ready with its new proposals and had decided to court the Midland Railway, a letter written by the temporary secretary Col Maude arriving at Derby on 7 August 1896, explaining the advantages expected by construction of the railway. On 17 September the Midland Board met with representatives from the local Company at Derby, and on the following day MR Solicitors were asked to continue negotiations with view to constructing a light railway from Skipton to Grassington, under the Light Railways Act, with support from the Midland Company. This however was not quite what the promoters had in mind since a light railway would be useless in the event of eventual expansion to the north. However the immediate purpose was to reach Grassington by rail and so no objections were raised, the Yorkshire Dales Railway bill going to Parliament in time for the 1897 Sessions.

This photograph was taken on the occasion of the cutting of the first sod on the Yorkshire Dales Railway on 7 June 1900. Back row standing, left to right: Edgar O. Ferguson (Engineer), J. Lambert (Director), John Scott (Director), W. A. Procter (Director), W. Morrison (Director), Col. W. W. Maude (Director) and W. H. Hutchinson (Contractor). Front row seated, left to right: J. B. Dewhurst, J. A. Slingsby, and Richard Wilson (Solicitor).

Grassington Museum Collection.

2. THE YORKSHIRE DALES RAILWAY – CONSTRUCTION, OPENING AND OPERATION

The deposited plans for the Yorkshire Dales Railway showed three railways:

No. 1 A curve 16 chains in length leaving the Skipton & Ilkley line near the north end of Haw Bank tunnel, and curving round to the north-west to make a junction with Railways No's 2 and 3.

No. 2 A continuation of No. 1, running for 8 miles 3 furlongs and 6¾ chains to Threshfield.

No. 3 A curve 33 chains in length from a junction with No's 1 and 2, to a termination by a junction with the MR in the direction of Ilkley at the west end of Embsay station.

From the deposited plans it was observed that the earth works were light, the ruling grade was 1in70 and the sharpest curve was of 12 chains radius. Powers were sought in the bill to enable the MR, NE or LYR to enter into agreements with the YDR as to construction and working of the railway. The estimated cost for construction was £44,828 to include an allowance of £3,000 for stations on railway No. 2. Further meetings with the Midland Railway produced an agreement dated 5 July 1897 whereby the Yorkshire Dales Railway was to complete construction and keep its line in a good state of repair at its own cost for 12 months excepting for the track and "other operating works" which were to be maintained by the Midland. The latter would staff, manage, maintain and work the line from its opening, they would install signalling, the cost of which was to be charged to the YDR, the Midland would provide locomotives and rolling stock. By this time of course the curve completing the triangle at Embsay (Line 3) had been deleted from the bill. The Midland were to operate an all year round passenger service of not less than four each way daily. There was also to be an early morning market train from Grassington to Skipton on Mondays and Saturdays. A Yorkshire Dales Revenue Fund was to be established to which would be credited, 1) the gross receipts of local traffic starting and terminating on the railway, 2) a mileage proportion due to the YDR from MR receipts in regard to through traffic passing over all or part of the YDR, 3) terminal allowances for through traffic arriving or finishing on the YDR, and 4) receipts due to the YDR from all other sources to include any tolls paid by other railway companies for use of the YDR line. The fund was to be divided half yearly on the basis of 60% to the Midland and 40% to the local Company.

On 6 August 1897 the YDR obtained its Act for the Grassington branch covering construction of proposed railways No's 1 and 2. The works were to be completed within a period of 5 years and running powers were granted into the MR Skipton station. Trains for Grassington would depart from the Ilkley platforms 5 and 6. Capital authorised was £45,000 with powers to borrow an additional £15,000 in loans, sums later increased by £9,000 and £3,000 respectively. Most of the capital was raised locally by the Directors although the Midland Railway held all the debentures at 3½% per annum. The promoters and first Directors were Sir Mathew Warton Wilson (Gargrave) – Chairman, James Lambert, George Kendal and John Scott (all of Skipton) and Willam Atkinson Procter (Rylstone). Colonel Maud (Rylstone) joined the Board on the death of Mr Kendal. In February 1898 Charles Walker (Skipton) was appointed Company Secretary. During 1898 the Company had fallen on hard times having failed to raise sufficient capital to construct the line and requested the Midland to take over, but the latter refused. The local Company contemplated its position and decided to carry on. Eventually agreement ws reached with Derby whereby the Midland would guarantee the capital necessary to build the Yorkshire Dales line. The Midland were to subscribe £5,000 providing the share capital subscribed locally would be increased to £40,000 and in addition to this would loan the YDR £15,000 at 3½% interest. The line was to be built as cheaply as possible and for operation initially on the one engine in steam

A typical construction scene on the YDR thought to be near Linton. Note the assortment of railway wagons, left to right: contractors, contractors 3-plank, and a MR 5-plank. The steam crane (upper right) runs on standard gauge track. An underbridge is being constructed but the exact location is unknown. A stationary steam boiler is visible on the left.

Grassington Museum Collection.

principle. By so doing economies could be made—no turntable being necessary, no passing loop at Rylstone and no carriage sidings at Grassington.

In January 1900 the YDR had appointed Edgar Ferguson (of Chesterfield) as Resident Engineer, he being well qualified having been responsible for the 17¾ mile Settle contract of the Settle & Carlisle Railway. Mr Ferguson had also been Consulting Engineer for all the Dales railway schemes from 1880 onwards. On 25 May 1900 William Haines Hutchinson (of Mansfield) was successful in his tender of £28.892 for construction of the line and he soon established his office at Holme Cottage, Embsay (opposite the entrance to Embsay station).

Hutchinson was, at the time of the construction of the Yorkshire Dales Railway, one of the youngest recognised railway contractors in the country. Born in 1868, he had entered service with the North Staffordshire Railway in 1885 and on expiry of his articles in 1888, was promoted to Assistant Engineer. In 1890 Hutchinson joined the Great Northern Railway and four years later joined Walter Binns & Sons, Contractor, (of Sutton-in-Ashfield) as Chief Engineer, actually working on the GNR Leen Valley Railway for which he had previously prepared drawings. It would appear that Walter Binns & Sons experienced financial difficulties during the completion of the Leen Valley extension, to the extent that Hutchinson purchased the plant and equipment and finished the contract himself.

On 25 May 1900 Hutchinson was awarded the contract for the construction of the Yorkshire Dales Railway. Of William Haines Hutchinson's life after the YDR contract, rather less is known. Presumably he had close contact with and often shared construction contracts with Baldry & Yerburgh, but a formal business arrangement was not achieved until 2 March 1910 when a new company called Baldry, Yerburgh & Hutchinson Ltd, was incorporated. Of the construction contracts, in which this new company was involved for the next 30 or so years, little is known, although it is certain that the concern survived until July 1942. At that time an entry in the Hunslet Engine Company records cryptically states that "We have recently purchased the B. Y. and H. plant".

But to return now to the Yorkshire Dales. The cutting of the sod ceremony was celebrated at Threshfield on 7 June 1900 with Walter Morrison MP officiating (in the absence of Sir Mathew Wilson, Chairman of the Company). The event was celebrated thus:

> "Order of Procession for the day. Leave Grassington at one o'clock prompt in the following order—1. Children, 2. Grassington Brass Band, 3. Councillors, overseers and public officials, 4. General public.
> Arriving at Threshfield at 1.30, leave the Old Hall Inn at 1.45 prompt as follows to the place of ceremony—1. Children, 2. Band, 3. Directors and Officials of the YDR, 4. Clergy and other Ministers of Religion, 5 Parish, Rural and Urban Councillors. Overseers of the floor, and other public officials (including school masters), and 6, the general public . . . On arrival at the Field Mr W. A. Procter will hand spade to Mr Morrison. Mr Hutchinson and Mr Ferguson will hand Barrow to Mr Morrison, and the latter gentleman will cut the sod . . . Col Maude will move, Dr Wilks second, and the Rev F. A. C. Share will support a Vote of Thanks to Mr Morrison". Then followed the National Anthem and the procession returned to Grassington.

It is recorded that construction occupied 350 men for two years and six weeks and the total cost of construction was £72,000.

The primary object of the Yorkshire Dales Railway was to afford improved communication to the inhabitants of Upper Wharfedale and prior to the coming of the railway coal and other goods was conveyed by road for distribution to local villages. Before the branch came into service public traffic between Grassington and Skipton was in the hands of "old time carriers carts and ancient buses" running two or three times a day each way. In addition there was a Mail coach which ran from Kettlewell to Skipton and back once a day. It was estimated that some 30,000 people and 30,000 tons of merchandise were carried annually by these conveyances and with an expected 100,000 tons per annum of coal, limestone and other minerals, the branch was expected to be quite profitable. For details of the locomotives employed on construction of the Yorkshire Dales Railway I am indebted to David M. Hird and also to the late B. D. Stoyel. Four locomotives are known to have been employed on the YDR contract:-

0-6-0ST. Built by Manning Wardle in 1876. Works No. 589. Inside cylinders 12in × 17in, 3ft 1⅜in driving wheels. Delivered new on 3 April 1876 to the Holwell Iron Company, Ashfordby, Melton Mowbray, Leicestershire, as "Victoria". Subsequently renamed "Holwell". Rebuilt by Holwell Iron Co in 1901 and then sold to Hutchinson and delivered by rail to Embsay. Hutchinson retained the name "Holwell" and added his fleet No. 11. Earlier in 1901 Hutchinson had ordered seven new locomotives from Manning Wardle (none of these worked on the YDR contract) and already owned the other three locomotives which are to be described. The new Manning Wardle locomotives were numbered by Hutchinson 4 to 10 respectively. How "Holwell" came to be numbered 11 is therefore perhaps satisfactorily explained. "Holwell" was one of four standard gauge Manning Wardle locmtives advertised for sale by auction in a sale of plant held in Colne on 24/25 September 1902 on completion of the Yorkshire Dales Railway and the concurrent Colne New Yard construction contract undertaken by Hutchinson for the Midland and Lancashire & Yorkshire Railway companies. Evidently "Holwell" was not sold as it was advertised again in December 1902. Later it passed into ownership of Whitaker Brothers, Contractors, and its subsequent history is unknown.

0-4-0ST. Built by Manning Wardle in 1895. Works No. 1303. Outside cylinders 10in × 16in. 3ft 0in driving wheels. Named "Kirkby". To Walter Binns, Contractor, and used by him on his Copley Hill, Leeds construction contract. Bought by Hutchinson when he assumed Binns' responsibilities for contract and plant on Binns' failure. Used on the Kirkby in Ashfield Langwith Junction contract, which ended 1901. Transferred to the Yorkshire Dales Railway job, where it remained until completion. Delivered to Colne August 1902 and included in the sale of plant there. It is certain that the locomotive was not sold as it appeared as an asset of the new concern of Baldry, Yerburgh & Hutchinson formed in March 1910. Later the locomotive was disposed of, and it spent some time with Flower & Everitt of Rainham.

0-6-0ST. Built by Manning Wardle in 1895. Works No. 1290. Inside cylinders 13in × 18in. 3ft 0in driving wheels. (WHH No. 3). New to Walter Binns, Contractor and subsequently passed to Hutchinson when he took over Binns' effects. Employed by Hutchinson on the Shirebrook No. 3 job and then to the Yorkshire Dales Railway contract. Later with H. Lovatt, Contractors, Stafford.

0-4-0ST built by Manning Wardle in 1895. Works No. 1304. Outside cylinders 10in × 16in. Named "Phillip". Similar early history to Manning Wardle 1303 and also included in the September 1902 sale of plant. Later with Manganeze Bronze & Brass Co Ltd, Ipswich.

In 1901 it was decided to obtain quotations for construction of the two stations i.e. Rylstone and Grassington. Since the Company was still in financial difficulties it was decided in December to accept a tender from the Portable Building Company of £173 for provision of a station at Rylstone, and £279 for that at Grassington. Both stations were to be "of a neat and novel design in wood work. The goods sheds are also to be made of wood, and the platforms are an entirely new type, made of timber on brick piers packed in between with dry stone and covered with limestone chippings".

In 1902 Sir Mathew Wharton Wilson, along with Col Maude and W. A. Procter, retired from the Board, being replaced by Walter

The only intermediate station on the YDR was at Rylstone, intended to serve the villages of Rylstone, Hetton, Bordley and Cracoe. The station had but one platform to serve the single track branch. View taken circa 1902 looking towards Grassington. Among the MR advertisements are services to Leeds, Bradford, London and Belfast. The "Suttons Seeds" advert "free by post and rail" is in a prominent position. Note the milk churns on the platform.

D. Binns Collection.

The station buildings at the Threshfield terminus were photographed shortly after the opening of the line. The name on the back of the seat under the canopy reads "Grassington". Note the cart and barrow and the neat lines of the wood station. The station-master's office is on the left, behind the wall-mounted clock.

D. Binns Collection.

Rylstone station on opening day 29 July 1902.   *Courtesy Mrs M. Chadwick, via D. M. Hird.*

Morrison MP, John Briggs (Bolton) and William Stockdale (Skipton). Major J. W. Pringle of the Board of Trade inspected the new works at Embsay Junction on 13 March noting that "a double junction has been laid in to the Midland line from the single track Grassington line, and a new cross-over road between the up and down lines of the Midland had been installed. A new 20 lever signal cabin known as Embsay Junction, had been constructed to control the points, and it formed a new block post on the Midland line". Along the branch most of the track was laid and both stations were nearing completion. A water tank costing £137-10-0 was erected at Grassington having been manufactured by Messrs Handyside. Tenders were being obtained for a goods shed at Grassington and discussions were under way for sidings for John Delaney to serve his quarry near Threshfield. Before the YDR could open for public service a further Board of Trade inspection was required and this was carried out on 9 July 1902 by Major Pringle. At Embsay Junction Pringle observed that a speed restriction of 15mph should be imposed around the curve. With regard to Crookrise Siding Pringle considered it necessary to request an undertaking to work the traffic at the siding with the locomotive at the Skipton end of the train—the reason for this due to the steep gradient. Although the goods shed at Grassington was not complete and station lamps and name-boards had not been installed, Pringle must have been well pleased with what he had seen and recommended the Board of Trade to allow the YDR to open for passenger traffic on 29 July 1902. The opening ceremony was to have been performed by

Lady Wilson but owing to a severe cold she was unable to attend and the ceremony was performed by her grand-daughter Mrs Rondell (of Gledstone).

The special lunch was served by Mrs & Mrs Metcalfe of the Old Hall Inn and comprised salmon, mayonnaise sauce, roast chicken/boiled chicken, york ham, roast beef, roast lamb and mint sauce, salad, jellies and cheese. At 4.00pm afternoon tea was served at the Old Hall Inn, Threshfield prior to departure of the Special Train for Skipton at 5.30pm.

The first Special Train had left Skipton at 12 noon carrying between 200 and 300 passengers. The locomotive was No. 1536, a Johnson 0-4-4T resplendent in crimson lake livery lined out in black and gold with polished brass numerals and fittings. It was decorated with flags and flowers and carried placards on each side which proclaimed "Success to the Yorkshire Dales Railway". The first train to arrive after the Official opening was pulled by another Johnson 0-4-4T with 10 carriages. It is interesting to note that more than 1000 people made the journey to Grassington on the opening day. The first single ticket from Skipton to Grassington was purchased by A. R. Stockdale, (a Skipton wine merchant) who had earlier obtained the first ticket from Skipton to Bolton Abbey and who was to obtain the last ticket between Skipton and Grassington in 1930. The first two tickets from Skipton to Rylstone were purchased by Gerald and Michael Maude.

In addition to the 12 noon special the following trains ran at ordinary fares on the opening day:

Opening day at Grassington 29 July 1902.   *Courtesy Mrs M. Chadwick, via D. M. Hird.*

The first train to arrive at Grassington station on the opening day was headed by Midland Railway Class 1P 0-4-4T No. 1536, resplendent in crimson lake and fully lined out in yellow and black. The banner on the side of the tank proclaims "Success to the Yorkshire Dales Railway"

D. Binns Collection.

Leave Skipton at	1.45	3.15	6.00	7.30
arr. Grassington	2.15	3.45	6.30	8.00
Leave Grassington	1.00	2.30	6.45	8.15
arr. Skipton	1.30	3.00	7.15	8.45

Calling at Rylstone station each journey.

Passengers for Grassington departed from platform 5 at Skipton station and travelled as far as Embsay Junction over the MR Skipton & Ilkley branch. At Embsay Junction the YDR forked northwards to cross the Skipton to Embsay road. A report in the *Railway Magazine* for 1902 noted that . . . "The route selected from the valley of the River Aire 356ft at Skipton, to Upper Wharfedale at Grassington (where the river is 550ft above the sea) runs its whole length through a trait of pastoral country which forms an open valley or dip between the high moors which separate the head waters and the lower reaches of the two rivers. These mountainous uplands culminate in Burnsall Moor at a height of 1600ft, but as the highest part of the dip is under 650ft above the sea, the fall to the terminus is very slight, as the line ends at a considerable height above the River Wharfe, between the villages of Threshfield and Linton, and ½ mile from Grassington."

Only enough land had been purchased for a single track railway and this consisted of second-hand 84lb/yd rails removed from parts of the Midland Railway where heavier rails had been installed. Along the 8 miles 53½ chains of route there was one public road level crossing (at Rylstone) protected by gates, 16 occupation crossing, 8 overbridges and 19 underbridges. The ruling grade was 1in75 and the sharpest curve (at Embsay Junction) was of 12 chains radius, with 20 chains elsewhere.

The first ordinary timetable showed 4 trains daily each way with an extra one on Mondays and Saturdays, the first in both directions was run as a mixed, then a passenger, a mixed, and a passenger. On Sundays there operated two passenger trains in each direction. By September 1902 the timetable was as follows:

From Skipton

5.50am	Goods Skipton–Crookrise (6.05), Green siding, near 6 mile post (6.15) Rylstone, arr. 6.20, dep. 6.30, Spencers sidings 6.42, Grassington arr. 6.50
8.45am	Mixed Skipton–Grassington
11.25am	Passenger Skipton–Grassington
3.00pm	Passenger Skipton–Grassington
5.55pm	Mixed Skipton–Grassington
8.00pm	Passenger Skipton–Grassington SATURDAY ONLY

From Grassington

7.00am	Mixed Grassington–Skipton (MONDAY EXCEPTED)
9.25am	Passenger Grassington–Skipton
12.05pm	Passenger Grassington–Skipton
3.45pm	Freight Grassington–Skipton calling at all stations and sidings
6.35pm	Passenger Grassington–Skipton
8.40pm	Passenger Grassington–Skipton SATURDAY ONLY

Grassington station circa 1905 looking towards Rylstone. Note the wood edging to the gravel covered platform. Loco water tank behind the carriages. The MR advertisement boards offer services to Morecambe, Ingleton, the Lake District and Edinburgh.

D. Binns Collection.

The first train to arrive at Grassington after the official opening comprised a MR 0-4-4T and ten carriages, with a five carriage close-coupled clerestory set next to the engine, six-wheelers behind.

D. Binns Collection.

MR 0-4-4T No. 1535 brings a train from Skipton into Grassington, comprising 4-wheel brake, 6-wheel carriage, 2 bogie carriages, 4-wheel brake, and at the rear the usual five coach close-coupled clerestory set. The date is circa 1905.

D. Binns Collection.

At Crookrise the points to the sidings were operated from a single lever ground frame by the train crew. The siding here served a small sawmill and was also used for stone. At Rylstone the level crossing was worked from a 6 lever ground frame protected in both directions by home and distant signals. Rylstone station was located in the middle of nowhere and intended to serve the villages of Rylstone, Hetton, Cracoe and Bordley. A platform some 300ft long was provided and the station building housed a booking hall, ladies waiting room and both ladies and gents toilets.

A report in the local newspaper indicated that "P. W. Spencer, the owner of kilns at Lothersdale (nr. Skipton) has taken (1902) quarrying rights at Swinden and is to build a number of kilns there". The new line passed close by an inn at Catchall (Swinden) where there was an old disused kiln, once justly celebrated for the quality of its lime. *Railway Magazine* stated "a huge new kiln is being erected. It resembled a blast furnace and looks strangely out of place between the fields and the moorlands, but it clearly proves the truth of the platitude that cheap communication creates traffic, and the district is likely to be enriched to the detriment of the wood and moorland scenery". According to Messrs Tilcon Ltd quarry development at Swinden under P. W. Spencer had commenced in 1899 and railway sidings at the quarry were completed in 1902 at the time of erection of the first kiln. A second kiln became operational in 1905 and between 1908 and 1914 a further four kilns were erected making six coal fired kilns in total. Access to Spencers sidings was obtained by two separate sets of points, each controlled by a single lever frame locked by the train crew.

During August 1902 P. W. Spencer had requested a passenger halt at his Swinden works, offering to build a 100ft long platform if the Midland Railway would stop its branch trains. Derby must not have thought much of this since the request was ignored.

The reasons for not taking the railway into the town of Grassington were several and the main one was the fact that a northern extension was then still hoped for and the terminus at Threshfield was planned with this in mind.

Another reason was the difference in levels which would have required high embankment and costly viaduct to carry the line into Grassington. Since the branch was not expected to carry a large volume of traffic and because the YDR were financially embarassed it was necessary to avoid expensive works and excessive construction costs which if incurred would reduce the chances of paid dividends. In olden times there were many small lead, copper and coal mines

working in Upper Wharfedale, but improved techniques and cheap transport from pits closer to the main centres of trade resulted in the end of these Dales industries. In fact all the ironworks from the old pit heads around Grassington had been dismantled prior to the opening of the Yorkshire Dales Railway in the impression that these pits could not be profitably worked. The coming of the railway was to change all this and it was reported in the local press that "William Delaney of Horton-in-Ribblesdale, has purchased mining rights for coal as well as lime getting rights on Threshfield Moor and will run a cable hauled tramway down to the terminus".

It was in fact John Delaney who had become the District's main distributor of coal and the owner of more than 1000 private railway wagons, some of which bearing his name, were still in evidence until the Second World War either unloading coal at Settle station, or marshalled in trains heading south carrying lime from his quarry at Horton-in-Ribblesdale to the steel mills of Sheffield. It was recorded that Delaney later opened a larger and more prosperous quarry at Threshfield and within 15 years had made his fortune. Delaney also had other quarries at Beecroft (along with a wagon repair depot), and at Broughton near Skipton.

In the event Delaney's quarry was situated at Skirethornes and during the early 1900s more than 100 men were employed there. Some coal was extracted from Threshfield Moor to fire the lime kilns. Delaney had requested siding accommodation of 11 chains at Grassington station and considerable tonnage of lime/stone was brought to the YDR rail-head by means of a 2ft 6in gauge steam powered endless rope-hauled tramway which passed beneath the Threshfield–Kilnsey road, running through open fields before terminating at a rail-head near Woodlands Terrace, Threshfield. In 1966 Hargreaves took over Skirethornes quarry by which time the endless rope-hauled tramway was out of action—the standard gauge railway being regarded as unsuitable for their type of trade. In 1979 ownership passed to Tarmac.

The terminus was at first named "Grassington" but in October 1902 was renamed "Grassington & Threshfield". It must be stated that immediately before closure the board simply read "Grassington". Two platforms were originally provided in the manner of a through station, which of course is just what the promoters hoped it would become. Although two platforms were built it was initially planned to use one only. Two ground frames controlled the run-round points and entry to the goods yard. For the first two years the Grassington branch was operated with a "train staff" on the one engine in steam principle but from 26 June 1904 the method of working was changed to the "Electric Tablet System" which allowed more than one train on the branch. The tablet was released from the machine by the action of the signalmen at Embsay Junction and Grassington, holding in simultaneously a plunger on their tablet machines. This plunger also operated the block bell and would be held in after the last beat on the bell accepting the train. When a tablet had been released and taken from the machine at Embsay Junction no other tablet could be removed until the free tablet had been placed in the machine at Grassington after arrival of the train, when if required, another tablet could be obtained. An official LMS map of 1938 states that the instruments were in the station office and it is possible they were moved there after withdrawal of the passenger service in 1930. On 26 June 1904 a passing loop was brought into use at Rylstone remaining as a passing place until withdrawal of the passenger service (by 1937 it was no longer shown as being a block post).

Commencing with the Summer 1910 timetable, a new through service for businessmen was introduced from Grassington to Bradford, reversing at Embsay Junction, leaving Grassington at 7.45am. On arrival at Embsay Junction the train headed towards the down main line starting signal clear of the cross-over points. A locomotive, which had earlier run light from Ilkley, waited on the up main line in front of the signal box. It than backed onto the train and hauled the Bradford portion away calling at Addingham and Ilkley. Meanwhile the front portion had left for Skipton arriving at 8.14am.

By May 1912 the following train services were in operation:

		Weekdays	(Sats)↓					
0	Skipton	8.41	11.40	1.10	3.12	4.38	5.55	7.35
7½	Rylstone	9.01	12.00	1.30	3.32	4.58	6.15	7.55
10¾	Grassington & Threshfield	9.09	12.08	1.38	3.50	5.06	6.23	8.03

Suns

Skipton	8.45	7.00
Rylstone	9.05	7.20
Grassington	9.13	7.28

		Weekdays	(Mons)↓					
0	Grassington & Threshfield	7.15	7.45	9.15	12.15	3.50	5.13	8.10
3¼	Rylstone	7.24	7.54	9.24	12.24	3.59	5.22	8.19
10¾	Skipton	7.41	8.14	9.41	12.41	4.16	5.39	8.36

Suns

Grassington & Threshfield	9.25	7.55
Rylstone	9.34	8.04
Skipton	9.52	8.21

In 1917 a change was made in the working and the locomotive which had previously run light from Ilkley, worked a passenger train to Bolton Abbey before continuing light to Embsay Junction (arriving 7.45am) and departing at 8.03am for Bradford. From 1 January 1918 the passenger train from Ilkley to Bolton Abbey was extended to Skipton from where a light engine was despatched at 7.47am for Embsay Junction to work the Bradford portion of the train from Grassington. This working then continued with minor alterations until withdrawal of the Grassington branch passenger service. Correspondence in the *Railway Magazine* for 1924 tells us that a Johnson Class 1 0-4-4T was generally used and that Kirtley double-frame 0-6-0 No. 2502 was often seen on the branch.

In the Summer of 1910 the MR had introduced a slip carriage for Grassington. This left Bradford Market Street station on the 5.10pm Residential Express to Morecambe, being slipped at Skipton and then attached to the 5.55pm train to Grassington, arrival 6.23pm. This service continued until 1917 when, in line with all other Midland slip coach workings, it was withdrawn. After this time there was no through working to Grassington in the down direction.

By 1911 The Yorkshire Dales Railway Officials were; Walter Morrison (Malham Tarn)—Chairman, Lieut Col William Wade Maude (Rylstone)—Deputy Chairman, John Briggs (Bolton), William Atkinson Procter (Rylstone), Major Richard Fooks (Gledstone), John Scott Jnr (Skipton), Matthew Amcotts Wilson (Eshton). Bankers—Bank of Liverpool Ltd (Craven Bank Branch, Skipton), Edgar O. Ferguson (Chesterfield) Engineer, and Richard Wilson (Skipton) Solicitor and Secretary.

The YDR still received 40% of the receipts from the Midland Railway, the remaining 60% being retained by Derby as operating expenses. From all sources (passengers, parcels, merchandise, minerals, livestock and sundries) the following receipts are extracted: 2nd half of 1910 £1516-6-5, 1st half of 1911 £1376-12-10, 2nd half of 1911 £1506-19-7. Passengers booked at Rylstone and Grassington were:-

At Rylstone—	2nd half of 1910	4643
	1st half of 1911	4006
	2nd half of 1911	4161
		12810

At Grassington—	2nd half of 1910	13098
	1st half of 1911	10888
	2nd half of 1911	13098
		37084

Numbers of passengers booked at stations on the Midland Railway to Rylstone and Grassington for the corresponding period were:-

To Rylstone—	2nd half of 1910	2659
	1st half of 1911	2538
	2nd half of 1911	2683
		7880

To Grassington—	2nd half of 1910	27594
	1st half of 1911	25527
	2nd half of 1911	26381
		79502

The line was used for excursion traffic from an early date, one typical example ran on Whit Tuesday 6 June 1911 when the Craven Naturalists & Scientific Association travelled over the YDR branch to Threshfield from whence they were driven forward to Buckden for a walk in the woods. Lunch at Starbotton was included in the estimated cost of 5/6d.

Further plans continued to be put forward for northern extensions to the Yorkshire Dales Railway and in May 1903 the Upper Wharfedale Light Railway proposed a line northwards from Threshfield to Buckden. The bill was withdrawn but tried again during 1907/8 and although supported by Skipton Urban District Council, failed, due mainly to opposition by the Midland Railway on the grounds that this scheme would damage any future YDR extension to the north.

A further ambitious proposal was born in 1904 when the North Yorkshire Dales Railway bill sought power for 12 railways totalling 51 miles of line. It was to join both the MR and LYR at Hellifield by two connecting loops, before passing eastwards where connection was to be effected with the YDR north of its Rylstone station. A further connection was to be made with the YDR at Grassington before the line continued to Kettlewell and Buckden. From there, two large viaducts and a 3100yd long tunnel near Bishop Dale would carry the proposed line towards West Burton eventually trailing beneath the NER Northallerton−Hawes branch near Spennithorne. The route was to continue to Catterick joining the Richmond branch south of Scorton station. This would have been an interesting line had it been built since electric propulsion was planned with generating stations at Threshfield, Barton cum Walden and East Hauxwell. Estimated cost of construction was £886,581. The bill was withdrawn by the promoters and was not heard of again.

Further proposals were still to come for northern extensions. In 1911 the North Yorkshire Dales Railway deposited a bill, the scheme of which was nearly identical to that of 1904 but with the portion between Hellifield and Grassington ommited, connection being end on with the YDR at Grassington. There was to be 33 miles of route via Kettlewell and tunnelling under Great Whernside into Coverdale with connection to the NER at Scorton. Running powers were sought over the NE to Darlington and Middlesbrough and over the YDR from Threshfield to Embsay Junction and over the MR to Skipton and Colne. The bill was opposed by the MR, NE and LYR and was dropped.

In November 1912 the North Yorkshire Dales Railway 1911 proposal was revived with minor alterations as to running powers and with the addition of a clause offering agreements with the NE, MR and YDR with reference to construction, maintenance and operation. Although the bill had its first reading in Parliament it was withdrawn and as far as can be traced no further proposals were to be made for northern extensions.

Grassington trains left Skipton from platform 5, the same one used by the Ilkley services. This somewhat "murky" picture shows the usual five coach MR close-coupled clerestory set followed by four 6-wheelers, and another clerestory bringing up the rear of this departing train. Notice the junction signal for trains arriving at platform 6 from the Ilkley direction.

Skipton Museum Collection.

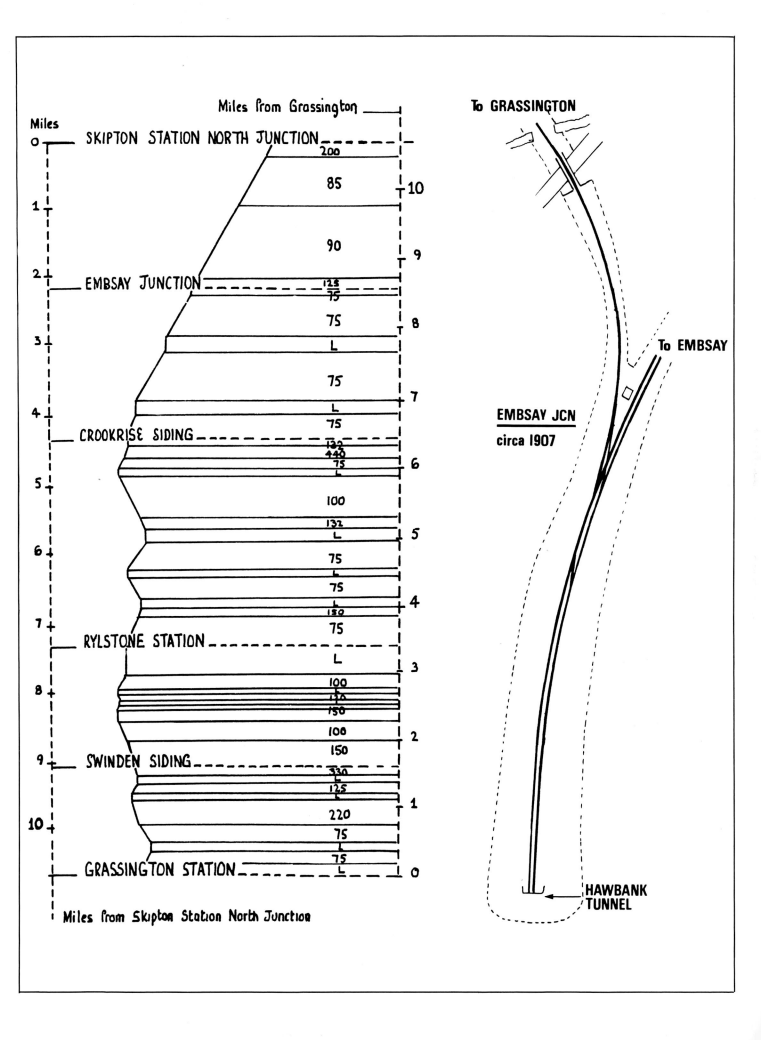

Miles from Grassington

Miles

SKIPTON STATION NORTH JUNCTION

0

200

85 — 10

1

90 — 9

2 EMBSAY JUNCTION — 125 / 75

75 — 8

3 L

75 — 7

4 L / 75

CROOKRISE SIDING — 132 / 440 / 75 — 6

100

5 132 — 5 / L

75

6 L / 75

4 L / 130

7 75

RYLSTONE STATION — L — 3

8 100 / 130 / 150

100 — 2

150

9 SWINDEN SIDING — 330 / 125

220 — 1

10 75

75

GRASSINGTON STATION — L — 0

Miles from Skipton Station North Junction

To GRASSINGTON

To EMBSAY

EMBSAY JCN
circa 1907

HAWBANK TUNNEL

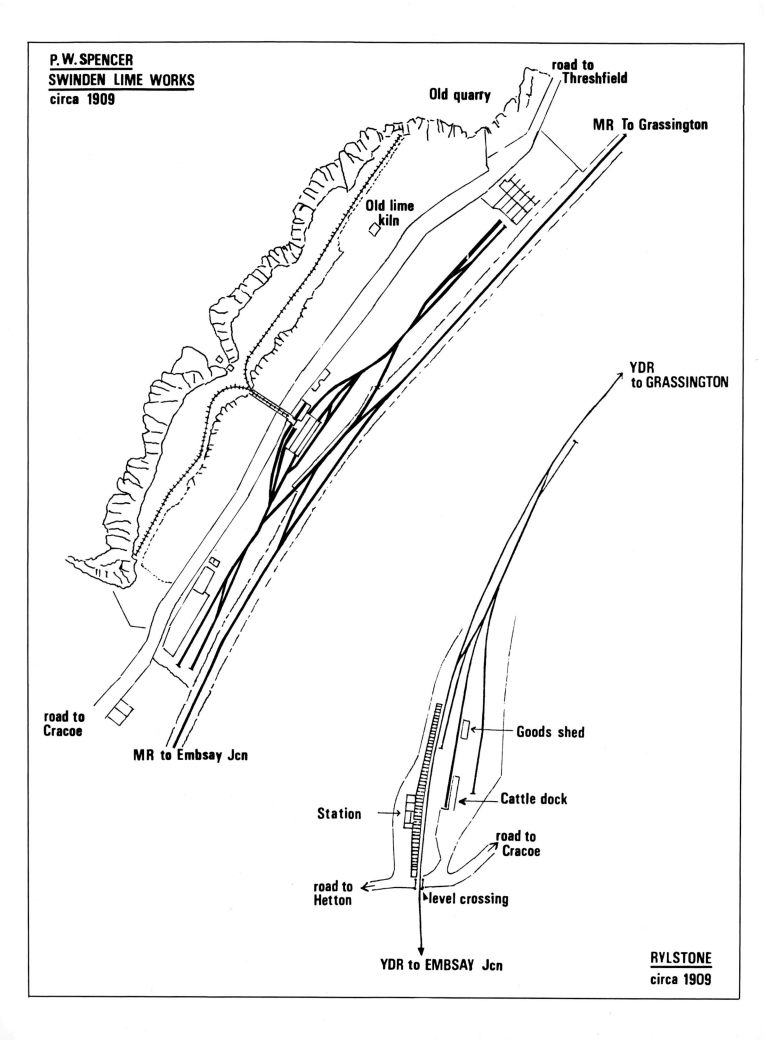

P. W. SPENCER
SWINDEN LIME WORKS
circa 1909

Old quarry

road to
Threshfield

MR To Grassington

Old lime
kiln

YDR
to GRASSINGTON

road to
Cracoe

MR to Embsay Jcn

Goods shed

Station

Cattle dock

road to
Cracoe

road to
Hetton

level crossing

YDR to EMBSAY Jcn

RYLSTONE
circa 1909

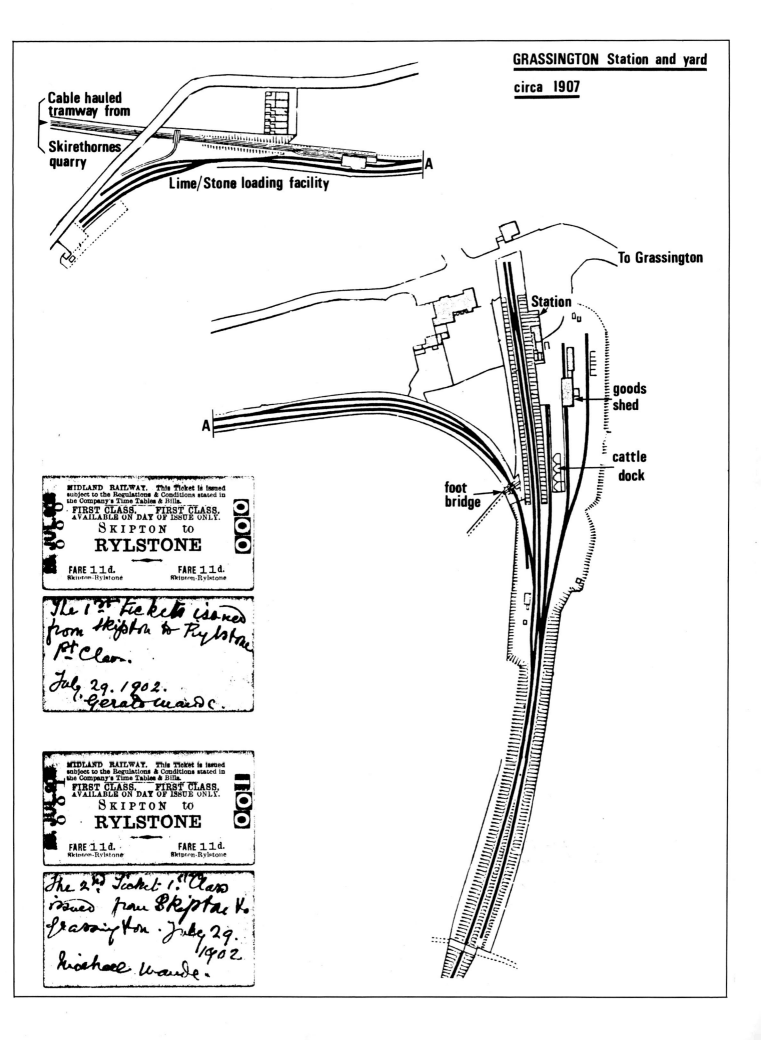

GRASSINGTON Station and yard
circa 1907

Cable hauled tramway from
Skirethornes quarry

Lime/Stone loading facility

A

To Grassington

Station

goods shed

cattle dock

foot bridge

A

MIDLAND RAILWAY. This Ticket is issued subject to the Regulations & Conditions stated in the Company's Time Tables & Bills.
FIRST CLASS.   FIRST CLASS.
AVAILABLE ON DAY OF ISSUE ONLY.
SKIPTON to
RYLSTONE
FARE 11d.   FARE 11d.
Skipton-Rylstone   Skipton-Rylstone

MIDLAND RAILWAY. This Ticket is issued subject to the Regulations & Conditions stated in the Company's Time Tables & Bills.
FIRST CLASS.   FIRST CLASS.
AVAILABLE ON DAY OF ISSUE ONLY.
SKIPTON to
RYLSTONE
FARE 11d.   FARE 11d.
Skipton-Rylstone   Skipton-Rylstone

YORKSHIRE DALES RAILWAY.

(SKIPTON TO GRASSINGTON).

Sir Mathew W. Wilson, Baronet,

and

Directors of the Yorkshire Dales Railway Company

request the honor of the presence of

A. E. Harker Esq.

at the Ceremony of Cutting the First Sod, to be performed by Walter Morrison, Esq., M.P., at the Terminus at Grassington on Thursday, June 7th, 1900, at 1-45 p.m. prompt.

CONVEYANCES WILL LEAVE SKIPTON RAILWAY STATION FOR GRASSINGTON AT INTERVALS DURING THE MORNING.

YORKSHIRE DALES RAILWAY.

Mr. Walter Morrison

and

Directors of the Yorkshire Dales Railway Company

request the honor of the presence of

Master Gerald Maude

at the Ceremony of the Opening of the Line by Lady Wilson, on Tuesday, July 29th, 1902.

The first train will leave Skipton Railway Station at 12.0 o'clock (noon), and return from Grassington at 5-30 p.m.

An early reply, to the Secretary of the Company, at Bank Buildings, Skipton, is desired, in order that all requisite arrangements may be made, details of which, with Railway Pass and Programme, will be forwarded.

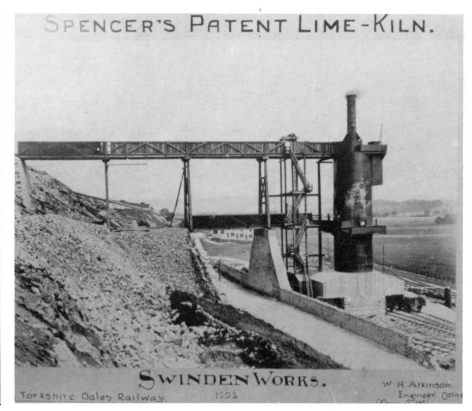

Yorkshire Dales Railway.

(SKIPTON TO GRASSINGTON.)

Opening of the Line

FOR PUBLIC TRAFFIC

BY

Lady Wilson,

TUESDAY, JULY 29TH, 1902.

= Railway Pass. =

(Skipton to Grassington, and Return.)

The first Train (Private Special) will leave Skipton Railway Station (Skipton and Ilkley Platform), at 12·0 (noon), returning from Grassington at 5·30 p.m.

In addition to the above, the following Trains will be run at ordinary fares:—

	p.m.	p.m.	p.m.	p.m.
Leaving Skipton at -	1·45	3·15	6·0	7·30
Leaving Grassington at -	1·0	2·30	6·45	8·15

Calling at Rylstone Station each journey.

Spencer's Patent Lime Kiln at Swinden was recorded on film when new in 1902. The Engineer in charge of construction was W. H. Atkinson, of Colne. The Grassington branch is visible to the right of the sidings which were also completed in 1902. The road in the foreground is that from Skipton to Threshfield. In the centre of the picture (beneath the lower bridge) can be seen a row of cottages under construction, these being for the use of quarry employees.

Grassington Museum Collection.

A birds-eye view of the Swinden plant between 1908 and 1914 with the Grassington branch railway passing behind the kilns. Note the extensive narrow-gauge tramway which fed the kilns.

Grassington Museum Collection.

Swinden Limeworks in July 1914 at the time of erection of No. 6 kiln.

Tilcon Ltd.

Yorkshire Dales Railway.

(SKIPTON TO GRASSINGTON.)

Opening of the Line

For Public Traffic,

BY

Lady Wilson,

TUESDAY, JULY 29th, 1902.

- *Programme.* -

12-0 (noon)—Special Train will leave Skipton Railway Station (Skipton and Ilkley Platform) for Grassington.

12-25—Arrive Rylstone Station.

Presentation of Key to LADY WILSON, by MR. WALTER MORRISON.

Public Opening of Rylstone Station, by LADY WILSON.

12-35—Special Train will leave Rylstone Station.

12-45—Arrive Grassington Station.

Public Opening of Grassington Station, and Declaration of the Opening for public traffic of the Yorkshire Dales Railway, by LADY WILSON.

Vote of thanks to LADY WILSON.

Addresses by MR. WALTER MORRISON and others.

1-30—LUNCHEON.—In Marquees in Field adjoining Station.—Entrance for Directors and invited friends from Station Yard only, and for the general public from the Field.

4-0—AFTERNOON TEA at the Old Hall Inn, Threshfield.

5-30—Special Train will leave Grassington for Skipton, calling at Rylstone.

The Upper Wharfedale recruits gathered at Grassington station prior to going to war on 21 September 1914.

Via D. M. Hird.

The Yorkshire Dales Railway Company was to survive until ended by the 1923 Grouping from which time it became part of the London, Midland & Scottish Railway. On 22 September 1930 the passenger service between Skipton and Threshfield was withdrawn, not unexpectedly, since, apart from holiday times, the bulk of passengers were businessmen travelling to and from Bradford and it was quite common for trains to carry no more than half a dozen passengers. This decline was due largely to road competition and the convenience of ½ hourly bus services between Grassington and Skipton. A further contributory factor was that Threshfield station was a mile from Grassington. From this time combined road and rail cheap day and season tickets were issued to Bradford from Grassington and Rylstone with bus services terminating/starting at Skipton railway station connecting with trains to Leeds and Bradford. Even at this late stage Col W. W. Maude wrote to Sir Josiah Stamp (President of the LMS) protesting against the decision and suggesting that an autocar might substitute for the present long heavy trains as it would be sufficient for the passengers, milk and parcels traffic on all ordinary days. "I hope I may have your assurance that the passenger traffic will be continued, not perhaps with so many trains per day, but with fewer trains better timed in accordance with main line traffic." The service was however not reprieved. Passenger excursion trains continued to run until the outbreak of the Second World War after which it was Easter Monday 1949 before another passenger train used the branch except perhaps for a hospital train to the Sanatorium at Grassington in the Autumn of 1944 when many of the southern sanatoria were being evacuated to the north because of flying bombs. On Easter Monday 6 June 1949 one of the first postwar excursions arrived carrying some 600 passengers from Bradford. This was followed by one from Leeds which had run via Ilkley and reversed at Embsay Junction. Hauled from Embsay Junction by 4F 0-6-0 No. 44277, this train carried some 1000 passengers arriving at Grassington one hour late. At night, No. 44277 worked the train back to Embsay Junction from where it was taken over by ex-MR Class 2P 4-4-0 No. 521. On 29 July 1951 a 10 coach excursion arrived at Grassington from Manchester, and on Bank Holiday Monday a Fowler Class 4 2-6-4T brought in 6 coaches from Leeds. On 13 August 1951 an excursion was run via Bolton Abbey reversing at Embsay Junction. The limited siding facilities at Grassington could get extremely congested at Bank Holidays as for example on Easter Monday 1952 when four excursions were dealt with. The first arrival was a 7 coach train from Blackburn hauled by 4F 0-6-0 No. 44438. The next from Bradford was ¾ hour late and came in with 4F 0-6-0 No. 43913 on 8 coaches. The train from Huddersfield and Leeds was over 1½ hours late and arrived behind 4F 0-6-0 No. 44007 hauling 10 coaches. All these trains were filled to capacity and an extra was put on from Skipton consisting of 4F 0-6-0 No. 43893 and 4 coaches from which alighted only six school children! Trouble was found in accommodating the 29 coaches in the limited space available and 8 were placed up the limeworks private siding. The Huddersfield train returned behind Ivatt 2-6-0 No. 43116 at 6.55pm. The other trains had gone earlier behind the 4F 0-6-0s. On 22 June 1952 a special left Manchester Victoria station at 9.43am bound for Grassington hauled by Hughes/Fowler "Crab" 2-6-0 No. 42820 hauling 10 carriages—at Grassington these were stabled in the quarry sidings. On the same day excursions from Leeds and Bradford were combined at Skipton from where they were hauled to Grassington by nothing larger than Ivatt Class 2 2-6-0 No. 46442—a type not normally considered powerful enough for use up the Grassington branch. On 19 April 1954 four well filled excursions traversed the Grassington branch—all hauled by 4F 0-6-0, from Leeds, Bradford, Huddersfield and one from the Central Division. On 4 February 1960 the District Engineers saloon passed over the branch

behind Ivatt Class 2 2-6-0 No. 46498. On 10 June 1957 three excursion trains arrived at Grassington—one of which was hauled by Ivatt light weight 2-6-2T No. 41284.

The signal box which controlled the Grassington terminus was of the usual Midland Railway timber construction and design, the operating floor being raised to first floor level and approached by a simple wooden staircase exposed to the elements. The box housed a 24 lever frame and all the signals were of Midland pattern with many lasting unaltered until closure.

Although the passenger service ceased in 1930 there was always enough goods traffic—principally coal and cattle feed to Grassington goods yard, and lime and limestone traffic from Swinden and Skirethornes—to sustain a branch service. Motive power for the branch was provided by Skipton mpd and until closure of the shed in April 1967 it was customary to roster a Fowler Class 4F 0-6-0, a number of which were fitted with tender back-cabs for work over the Settle & Carlisle line, but which were of equal comfort for the enginemen on the exposed Grassington branch.

During the 1950s and probably for many years before that, the box was worked by two Porter-Signalmen who spent a large part of their time in the goods warehouse unloading bags of cattle food or fertiliser. When either of these two men were off sick or on holiday, the job was done by a relief signalman, many of whom felt that their job was signalling and not humping hundredweight bags of fertiliser around! The Station Master Mr Len Huff may have had to crack the whip at times! One could have sympathy with the relief men who would sometimes end their shifts looking like the millers ghost, being covered from head to foot in fertiliser dust.

The box was closed in September 1962 and the line then reverted to one engine in steam operation. All signals were then removed and the points converted to hand operation. On 9 September 1962 "Crab" 2-6-0 No. 42705 hauled what was probably the last excursion prior to removal of the signalling. However, the signal box was destined to survive. At that time the Upper Wharfedale Fell Rescue Association had equipment storage facilities in a former railway carriage situated on the station forecourt, but in 1962 negotiations opened for the purchase of the unused signal box still sited in its original position to the south of the station. Agreement was reached in October of that year and the box was moved bodily after the four corner posts supporting the structure were sawn through and all the window frames and glass had been removed. The following report is extracted from the *Craven Herald & Pioneer* for 19 October 1962:

"The Upper Wharfedale Fell Rescue Association, at Grassington are used to tackling difficult jobs. They have rescued scores of people from caves, potholes, old lead mines, mountain slopes and precipices, and they have saved the lives of numerous animals marooned in dangerous spots. On Sunday they took part in their biggest operation—judged by sheer weight. This was the removal of a two-tier signal box (as big as a house) in one piece, a distance of a quarter of a mile into the forecourt of the Grassington railway station. The signal box is now their new headquarters. Removal operations took six hours. Sixty years old, the signal box is a stout wood building, with a tiled roof. It is 25ft high, 22ft long and 13ft 7in wide, and it weighs just over eight tons.

Members of the Fell Rescue Association did all the labouring and preparatory work, but a professional contracting firm, George Cohen & Sons & Co. Ltd., Stanningley, Leeds, did all the crane work, and also loaned a low loader to transport the signal box. . . .The job of moving the signal box took all morning and part of the afternoon. Mr. Joshua Swithenbank, a quarry engineer at Threshfield, who is President of the Fell Rescue Association, was the officer in change. Considerable skill was

demanded of the crane operator, Mr. Joe Walker of Kirkstall Road, Leeds. He told a *Craven Herald & Pioneer* reporter that although the crane was capable of lifting 22 tons, the 8 tons signalbox was quite heavy enough, having regard to the length of the jib required and the difficult angle at which some of the work had to be done. 'But the chief problems have been the bulkiness of the signal box and the great care needed to protect the upper structure which is rather fragile, he said.

Apart from sections of eaves troughing, the signal box was undamaged. So that the building could be airborne, steel hawsers were fixed to wooden sleepers underneath. The sleepers were part of the foundations, and they proved in excellent condition despite the fact that they had been in the ground since 1902. Removal operations were complicated and greatly prolonged by the fact that four sets of metals on the permanent way had to be crossed twice. Driving the low loader across railway lines called for coolness and resource. Once, the signal box leaned over at such a precarious angle that it looked certain to fall off the vehicle, but the crew never showed the slightest apprehension."

So it was that the former railway carriage was disposed of and the signal box was installed in the station yard.

The Winter of 1963 was the worst since 1947 and Wharfedale bore rather more than its share that year. Freight services in 1963 consisted of two trip workings from Skipton leaving at 10.15am and 2.15pm, and returning from Grassington at 12.30pm and 3.30pm. Embsay Junction signal box was open on a one shift basis from 9.45am to 4.45pm. The Grassington branch was very exposed and snow blowing off the surrounding fields made the task of keeping it open extemely difficult. On the morning of 21 January, two class 4F 0-6-0 engines coupled tender to tender with a large snowplough at each end set off from Skipton and succeeded in opening the line through to Grassington by 12.30pm. The Skipton to Grassington road had been blocked since the previous day and the afternoon freight trip carried a few passengers in the goods brake van. Things then improved slightly and the line remained open until 6 February when after further heavy snow and strong winds both rail and road access to Grassington was

In this picture four excursion trains were stabled in the limited siding space at Grassington. Some carriages have even been stored in the siding (off to the left) which was normally used for loading lime from Skirethornes quarry. The extent of the Grassington layout can be seen in this picture with goods shed, cattle-dock, passenger station, signal box and footbridge over the limeworks siding. M. Feather.

A Class 4F 0-6-0 at Grassington terminus on excursion train C920 from the former LMS Central Division, probably originating in Manchester. The main station building is seen on the left and is the original portable structure erected for the opening in 1902. M. Feather.

A Manchester–Grassington excursion (IT60) headed by Hughes/Fowler "Crab" 2-6-0 No. 42873, near Rylstone on 7 August 1961.

G. Dingle.

A Souvenir of the opening of the campaign to secure the eventual preservation of the Grassington Branch Railway

Embsay and Grassington Light Railway
EMBSAY
TO
GRASSINGTON & THRESHFIELD
2nd Class Fare 3/-
For conditions see over

Autumn, 1968
SKIPTON

Price 6d.

cut. Two engines with plough at each end left Skipton at 10.20am and opened the line through to Grassington but on arriving back at Embsay Junction had to return immediately to Rylstone as snow blowing off the fields was rapidly closing the line again at this point. The morning goods was cancelled but the afternoon trip succeeded in reaching Grassington. On the return journey it became stuck in drifts at Rylstone. After uncoupling the engine and charging the drift several times, a way was forced through and the train passed Embsay Junction at 5.20pm some two hours after leaving Grassington. The next day (7 February) the line was again reported blocked at Rylstone and a single 4F engine and plough was sent out but became stuck in drifts about 1½ miles before reaching Rylstone. Another locomotive was sent to the rescue and both returned to Skipton at 5.30pm having failed to open the line. The next morning two locomotives with ploughs at each end set out from Skipton passing Embsay Junction at 9.20am but could not get beyond Rylstone despite charging the drifts many times. They returned to Skipton for refreshment and set out for a second attempt at 1.30pm, this time succeeding in forcing a way through to Grassington by 4.15pm. One freight trip managed to get to Grassington and back the next day, which was a Saturday. There were no trains on Sunday, and snow blowing off the fields closed the line once again with the result that on Monday 11 February a report was received that the morning goods was stuck in drifts at Rylstone, and worse, a loaded coal wagon was derailed. The tool vans arrived from Skipton and after rerailing the coal wagon the goods managed to struggle through to Grassington and successfully return to Skipton. All went well for the next two days owing to a moderation of the wind, but on the afternoon of 14 February the snow struck again and the return goods from Grassington came to a stand in a large drift about a mile on the Skipton side of Rylstone level crossing. Two engines were sent to the rescue but only managed to derail three wagons in attempting to free the train. After many abortive attempts to rerail the three wagons the train had to be left on the single line and the three engines returned to Skipton passing Embsay Junction at 2.30am on the morning of 15 February. No snowplough was available on the 15th and the train was left blocking the branch. On 16 February a rescue operation was mounted and succeeded in rerailing the wagons

and removing the train to Skipton. The weather on the next day, Sunday 17 February, was appalling with heavy snow overnight drifting in gale force freezing winds. Snowploughs worked on the Grassington branch from 9.00am to 5.00pm in the hope that the next days morning goods would be able to get through. Traffic was heavy on the branch at this time with up to 40 empty high goods wagons plus 2 or 3 loaded coal wagons being taken up each morning. Monday morning 18 February saw a large train of empties assembled at Skipton for the Grassington trip and in an attempt to give the train more power to punch its way through, a Stanier class 5 4-6-0 was coupled in front of the train engine which was 4F 0-6-0 No. 44468. The train left Skipton at 10.48am and passed Embsay Junction in fine style, but disaster struck just short of Rylstone where the inevitable drifts had built up overnight. The two locomotives were brought to a stand and uncoupled from the train to charge the drifts, with the result that both derailed. Assistance was sent for and an engine was coupled to the rear of the train taking it back to Skipton. Meantime the Holbeck steam crane had been summoned and this arrived at 2.20pm hauled by 4F 0-6-0 No. 44099. One locomotive was rerailed and brought back to stand at Embsay Junction while the crane returned for the second engine. A lot of difficulty was encountered in rerailing this and it was the early hours of the next morning, 19 February, before it was removed to Skipton. Further difficulties were experienced during the next few days but with an easing of the weather the trains managed to get through.

From 10 February 1964 the Grassington branch freght workings were reduced from two to one each way on weekdays, departing from Skipton at 1.00pm and returning from Grassington at 3.30pm Mondays to Fridays. On Saturdays the timing were Skipton depart 10.00am, returning from Grassington at 12.30pm. The Saturday workings were later discontinued. From mid 1966 Standard Class 4 4-6-0s started to take over the branch freight workings and Nos. 75011/19/27/40/42/48/58 were among those noted being the last steam locomotives to work the branch. After closure of Skipton engine shed in April 1967, the same Standard Class 4 4-6-0s continued to work the Grassington branch from Leeds, Rose Grove and Carnforth sheds. Steam working ended in July 1968.

An ex-MR 4F 0-6-0 with tender back-cab was seen crossing the Leeds & Liverpool canal on the climb out of Skipton on the one-time Ilkley branch.   *M. Feather.*

Amidst rural surroundings, ex-MR Class 4F 0-6-0 No. 43999 trundles a Grassington bound freight through Rylstone in the early BR period. Note the tender back-cab, a feature of many Skipton based 4F locomotives. There were no turning facilities at Grassington and the return journey was made tender first.   *M. Feather.*

One of the earliest visits of a diesel locomotive on the branch was that of English Electric Type 4 No. D346, which on 15 November 1965 ran through from the Ilkley direction (being the last through working over that line) to test the Class on the branch sidings for clearance etc. Since the 1950s and early 1960s a few passenger excursion trains have traversed the Grassington branch. In 1964 the RCTS ran a diesel locomotive hauled special to Grassington and back. Five years later the Embsay & Grassington Railway Preservation Society hired a dmu for a round trip Skipton−Grassington−Skipton and this was indeed the last passenger train to run into Grassington Station. The following is extracted from the *Craven Herald & Pioneer* for 2 August 1969:

"There was an air of nostalgia, on Wednesday evening, as the last passenger train from Skipton to Grassington, a two-coach diesel unit, run by the Yorkshire Dales Railway Society, travelled to Grassington and back. It was 67 years ago that the first passenger train of the Yorkshire Dales Railway Company ran on the route, on July 29, 1902, and travelling on Wednesday evening were two people who rode on that first passenger train. They were Mr. J. C. Scott, whose father Mr. J. Scott was a director of the Yorkshire Dales Railway Company, and Mrs. J. Ellis, of Grassington, whose husband was a porter at Grassington Station. Mr. J. C. Scott was also present at the cutting of the first sod of the railway from Skipton to Grassington. About 130 people travelled on the last train, and apart from officials and members of the Yorkshire Dales Railway Society, they included rail enthusiasts from near and far. . . .

For once, speed was of no concern to the passengers, a large number of whom were armed with cameras to record the occasion, as the train travelled along at about 10mph, a limit laid down by the Ministry of Transport, because of the deterioration of the line, especially from Swinden Lime Works to Grassington. Along the route people gathered to watch and take photographs of the train, and a small crowd assembled at Grassington Station to welcome it . . . Driver of the train was Mr. Harry Robinson, of Sutton, who was accompanied by Mr. T. Worrall, assistant station manager at Skipton. Guard was Mr. George Hartley, of

The same train as pictured at the bottom of page 23 was recorded further along the branch en-route from Rylstone to Grassington.

M. Feather.

A Skipton-based Class 4F 0-6-0 with tender back-cab was captured on film at Grassington in the 1950s. The spur curving to the right of the picture was used to load limestone from Skirethornes quarry. Note the MR finials atop the two nearest signals, one of which is still lower quadrant.

D. Joy.

Skipton, who was kept busy operating the level crossing gates at Rylstone, going and coming back from Grassington.

The section of the railway line between Swinden Limeworks and Grassington Station is to be dismantled, but the Swinden to Skipton length will not only remain but will be in daily use for the carriage of freight, comprising limeworks products. There will be no delay in introducing the new regime; in fact the buffers will be installed at Swinden on Monday."

The official date for total closure of Grassington & Threshfield Station was given as 11 August 1969.

The last 1½ miles from Swinden limeworks to Grassington Station closed completely on 22 August 1969. Following this the rails were lifted and control and communication equipment removed. At Grassington, British Rail was left with a strip of land it could not use in an area in which it did not operate. The original wooden station buildings erected at a cost of £279 in 1902 were still standing, but in a rapidly deteriorating condition and these were eventually demolished in the mid 1970s and the station site, goods yard and forecourt sold for housing development in 1973.

With the closure of the line at Grassington and gradual delapidation of the station premises, notice was served that the site occupied by the Upper Wharfedale Fell Rescue Association could not be guaranteed, a move was therefore required and the signal box was dismantled in late 1972.

BR Standard Class 4 4-6-0 No. 75019 was recorded on film near Crookrise enroute to Skipton with a train load of stone from Swinden.

D. Binns.

Rylstone level crossing circa 1967, looking towards Embsay Junction.

D. Binns Collection.

Rylstone level crossing circa 1967 showing the gates and ground frame cabin.

D. Binns Collection.

In 1964 the Railway Correspondence & Travel Society ran a special over the Grassington branch. This was photographed leaving Swinden behind a Class 24 diesel on its return to Skipton.

D. Binns.

Photographed in 1950, Bridge No. 33 carried the Linton road over the railway, near Catchall at 6 miles 65 chains. At the time of construction the County Council would not allow the road to be altered in level or diverted, and this necessitated the making of a short deep cutting through limestone over which the road was carried.

D. Ibbotson.

Ings Bridge (No. 37) was indeed a "one-off" carrying an ancient footpath from Linton to Threshfield across the line. Top photo: with track in position in 1950, and bottom: May 1983 after the track had been lifted.

D. Ibbotson (both).

Both the BR Standard Class 4 4-6-0 No. 75058 and the railway at Threshfield were near to the end when this picture was taken. The station name-board reads "Grassington". Behind the locomotive is Baxter's confectioners shop which presumably would have had to be demolished if the northern extension had been built.

D. Binns Collection.

Opposite page: Three views of the interchange facilities used by Skirethornes quarry. Top: looking towards Threshfield. Middle: looking towards Grassington station. Stone was brought from Skirethornes quarry to this loading point by means of an endless rope railway, passing beneath the Threshfield—Grassington road and the Threshfield—Kettlewell road by means of small cuttings and bridges. The rope hauled tubs operated until shortly before the demise of the branch. Note the ramp up which the narrow gauge tubs were hauled for transfer of stone to standard gauge rail wagons. Bottom: with just enough space to take two rail wagons, coal was unloaded under cover. D. Joy (all).

Grassington & Threshfield signal box in working condition. W. A. Camwell.

This view shows the footbridge which spanned Delaney's siding, the track beneath it leading to facilities used for loading stone from Skirethornes quarry. The footbridge was later demolished and replaced by a stile at track level. In the background can be seen the wooden goods shed. D. Joy.

Grassington station in the later years when still open for goods traffic.

D. Joy.

These two photographs are included with the railway modeller in mind and show the rear of the station from two different angles as it looked in 1966.

D. Thorne.

More modellers views. This structure was located at the Rylstone end of Grassington station building—see top picture on page 30.

D. Thorne.

In October 1962 the Grassington signal box was removed from its original site to one in the station yard. "The 600 Group" provided the transport and the expertise to move the box to its new home for its new owners, The Upper Wharfedale Fell Rescue Association.

D. Thorne.

Grassington goods shed in 1966.

D. Thorne.

The opposite end of Grassington goods shed in 1966.

D. Thorne.

The office end of Grassington goods shed in 1966.

D. Thorne.

Bottom left: Grassington goods yard crane in 1966.

D. Thorne.

The box as it looked in June 1966 in its capacity as a Rescue Post of the Fell Rescue Association. Note that the name "Grassington & Threshfield has been retained on the cabin front.

D. Thorne.

From its earliest days at the turn of the century, Swinden Quarry has been concerned primarily with the production of lime. Originally, breaking and filling was carried out by hand with a labour force of over 60 men. Horse-drawn skips, clattering hand shovels, aching backs and billowing smoke—these were the features of quarry life at the time of the original coal-fired kilns. Indeed this lasted right up to 1948 when new crushing and screening plant was installed along with mechanisation of stone production. In 1965 Swinden quarry was acquired by the LSM Group who two years later replaced the 6 coal-fired kilns with 2 oil-fired units. At the same time new secondary crushing and screening plant was installed. At this time roadstone, ballast etc, was shipped direct by road, or loaded by conveyor into railway wagons. the newly installed kilns were supplied by conveyor and lime was then loaded onto rail wagons for delivery to the South Durham Steel & Iron Company, West Hartlepool. Other lime was loaded into wooden wagons for delivery to the Skinningrove Iron Company on the North Yorkshire coast, but since wood wagons were in short supply delays were resulting. As far as can be traced, shunting was carried out by a dumper truck but probably about the beginning of 1967 the first standard gauge industrial locomotive arrived at Swinden—this was No. 603, an 0-4-0 diesel, Ruston Hornsby Works No. 252684—a machine of approx. 165hp—thought to have been purchased secondhand from the Midlands.

When services were discontinued between Ilkley and Embsay Junction there was no need to retain Embsay Junction signal box, which closed on 6 July 1969. Following later singling of the track between Embsay Junction and Skipton, the branch to Swinden reverted to one train only operation. Later, to permit more than one train on the branch, the electric token system was again installed.

In 1970 Tilcon Ltd was formed with the quarry at Swinden passing to the new organisation. In 1971 Tilcon secured a British Steel Corporation contract to supply lime to their works. The "Swinden Project" as it became known, came into being in 1970 and was an ambitious scheme aimed at more than doubling the output of limestone. This involved the installation of new stone crushing, screening and handling plant, the erection of new lime kilns, the re-routing of the public highway to the opposite (low) side of the quarry, the expansion of rail loading facilities, tree screening and landscape works, and extensive pollution control measures. A North Sea gas pipe line was required and there was to be a new concrete block plant. Work began at the end of 1970 with the clearing of land in the quarry to make space for the new plant. In the excavation of the new quarry Tilcon Ltd decided to preserve the wings of the old workings in order to obscure extraction from public view as far as possible.

First of the major plant developments was the new primary impact crusher with its associated vibrating screens and conveyors which, in conjunction with the existing plant, increased the output potential of the quarry to about 900 tonnes per hour. 25 tonne dump trucks feed the crusher. These trucks are loaded at the face by a 4¼ cubic yard excavator and a 6 cubic yard loading shovel. The processing plant is semi-automated and production, grading and loading are operated from panel switches in the control room at the heart of the quarry. The two new kilns, the first of their type to be installed in Britain, each incorporate a vertical preheating system with shaft cooler and horizontal rotary section. In addition, there is some 2500 tonnes of storage capacity in silos. The two giant rotary kilns are refractory-lined steel tubes, horizontally inclined and rotated on rollers; 36 metres in length, they each contain some 800 tonnes of refractory bricks and are heated to 1200°C. A whole week is required to cool them down to normal temperature. North Sea Gas was the selected fuel system because it provided a pollution-free discharge to atmosphere. The pipe-line, specially laid from Skipton over a ten mile length, eliminates road congestion by oil tankers—another important environmental consideration in planning the development. The two

This interesting view is unfortunately not dated but shows a narrow gauge diesel locomotive being either lifted into or out of the quarry workings. Below is the original main road from Skipton to Threshfield. Any information concerning this photograph would be welcomed.

Grassington Museum Collection.

Bridge No. 32 carried the Skipton—Threshfield road over the railway prior to the 1970 Swinden project being completed. This circa 1952 view was taken from the Cracoe end looking towards Swinden. The main road passed over this bridge and ran between the aggregate and lime plants, but as part of the modernisation project the road was diverted to completely by-pass the quarry.

D. Ibbotson.

SWINDEN WORKS/QUARRY

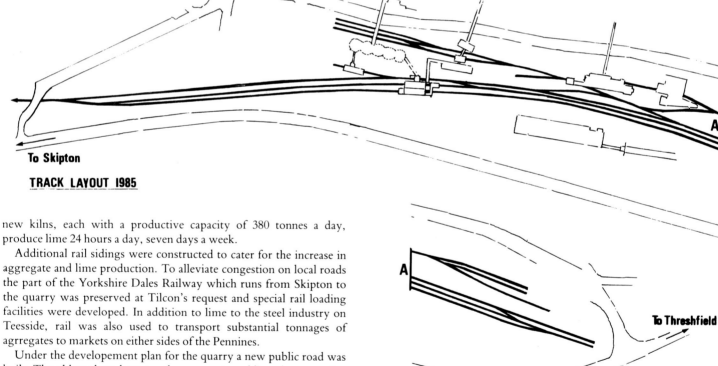

To Skipton

TRACK LAYOUT 1985

A

A

To Threshfield

new kilns, each with a productive capacity of 380 tonnes a day, produce lime 24 hours a day, seven days a week.

Additional rail sidings were constructed to cater for the increase in aggregate and lime production. To alleviate congestion on local roads the part of the Yorkshire Dales Railway which runs from Skipton to the quarry was preserved at Tilcon's request and special rail loading facilities were developed. In addition to lime to the steel industry on Teesside, rail was also used to transport substantial tonnages of agrregates to markets on either sides of the Pennines.

Under the developement plan for the quarry a new public road was built. The old road ran between the aggregate and line plants creating difficulties for motorists and lorry drivers alike; the new road completely by-passes the whole of the quarry operational area to the benefit of both—the first significant improvement since the introduction of turnpike status to the Cracoe—Skipton road in 1853!

By 1973 the development project had been completed and there was full production from both kilns. The extensive Swinden lime works are of course now the sole reason for the continued existence of the remaining section of the Grassington branch and a section of the Ilkley—Skipton branch from Embsay Junction to Skipton.

Sole traffic between Skipton and Swinden are the block trains of specially designed hopper wagons which are painted in Tilcon livery. Several types have been used and in January 1988 there were two

different types of hoppers in service. At one time a block of British Rail "BRT" type wagons was in use. The only exceptions to the block trains are the once yearly visit of the weed-killing train, an occasional inspection trip, and driver training, for which a 2 car dmu is used. Late in 1987 a 100 ton bogie tank was hauled to Swinden behind a Class 47 diesel locomotive. Bogie ballast hoppers have also been to Swinden. The earlier block trains were hauled by pairs of Class 25 diesels or by a single Brush type 47, a single type 40, 45 or 46. It is not known if these earlier block trains were the subject of speed trials or it may have been simply a case of over enthusiastic drivers, but on more than one occasion a Brush type 47 was seen hurtling down grade towards Skipton at something like 50+ mph with 32 Tilcon hoppers! Eventually speeds settled down and trains have been operated as required to destinations such as Hull Dairycoates and Leeds Marsh Lane, current motive power being provided by pairs of Class 31 diesel locomotives, usually on 32 or 34 loaded hoppers. It is interesting to note that stone from Swinden was shipped by rail to Goole for use in construction of the Humber Bridge.

In the 1980s the Embsay based Yorkshire Dales Railway ran several 2 car dmu excursions from Skipton to Rylstone and back. In 1983 on quite the rainiest day of the year an interesting working took place between Skipton and Rylstone when a special from the London area traversed the branch hauled by a type 45 and a type 47—one locomotive at each end of the train. In the following year on an equally wet day a special from Swansea called the "Rylstone Rambler" ran over the branch headed by a type 31 at the front of the train and assisted by two more 31s at the rear. Both these trains had restaurant cars—surely the only occasions such vehicles had been seen on the branch beyond Embsay Junction.

Shunting at the enlarged rail-head at Swinden has been in the hands of 3 ex-BR 0-6-0 diesel locomotives:

Class 08 English Electric 400HP 0-6-0 No. 08054 (ex-13067)
Class 11 English Electric 350HP 0-6-0 No. 12083
Class 12 English Electric 350HP 0-6-0 No. 15231 (cut up May 1985)

On 9 February 1988 another first took place when a new type of two car self propelled track recording unit, based on the "Sprinter" bodyshell, travelled the Grassington branch to check standards on the branch. In June 1990 the weed-killing set was seen on the branch. The locomotives (a type 20 on each end of the train), are owned by Hunslet Barclay. The train comprises 3 45-ton water tankers, one spray coach, one chemical storage coach, a workshop and domestic coach, and a dormitory coach—these being owned by Schering.

The rail layout as it is now with a pair of Class 31 diesel locomotives coupled to a train of Tilcon hoppers. View taken from Bridge No. 32 looking towards Grassington. The new road by-passing the quarry is visible on the right.

P. Hatherley.

Swinden plant from the Grassington end of the line. One of Tilcon Ltd diesel shunters is visible in this 1988 picture.
P. Hatherley.

Part of the modernised Tilcon plant showing a different series of hoppers once used on the branch.
S. Murley

Prior to the introduction of Class 31 diesels branch services were worked by pairs of Class 25 diesel locomotives. Two of these were photographed climbing out of Skipton, crossing the Leeds & Liverpool canal with a train of empty hoppers for Swinden.

J. Winkley.

A scene typical of the Grassington branch—a pair of Class 31 locomotives No's 31.273 and 31.238 photographed at Skipton, having just come down the branch with hoppers from Swinden.
P. Hatherley.